# The Maple
# Thanksgiving

*Written by Joseph Bruchac*
*Illustrated by Anna Vojtech*

Rio Seco
School

CelebrationPress
*An Imprint of ScottForesman*

Mary Elm walked along the road to school. It was March, but it was still cold. Mary was happy because it was time for the thanksgiving. She looked up at the bare branches of the maple trees and smiled.

When Mary got to school her best friend, Alice Mohawk, was waiting for her. Alice waved.

"Can you smell it?" Alice shouted.

Mary lifted up her head. It was a sweet smell — the smell of maple sap being cooked into syrup.

They walked together into the classroom. Through the window they could see the sugarhouse.

Mr. Elm, Mary's uncle, was out there. Every year he helped make maple syrup for the school.

Earlier in the week, the children had gathered sap from the trees around the school. Now Mr. Elm poured the sap into the big metal pan. Then he watched the fire. The sap bubbled. It steamed. As it cooked, it smelled sweeter and sweeter.

There was a picture of a big maple tree on the blackboard. "What time of year is this?" Miss Mitchell asked.

"It's the time to thank the maple trees," Mary said.

"That's right," Miss Mitchell said. "Why do we thank the maples?"

10

"It's our Iroquois way," Dennis Tarbell said. "The maples give us syrup. So we give them thanks."

"Very good," Miss Mitchell said. "Other people have just one Thanksgiving. We Iroquois have many thanksgivings. At the end of winter, we thank the maples."

At noon, everyone went out to the sugarhouse. Each child put clean snow into a cup. Then Mr. Elm picked up a big spoon and poured hot sap onto the snow in their cups.

"Niaweh," Mary said. "Thank you, and thanks to the maple trees."

12

Mary tasted the maple syrup in her cup.
It was cold now. It tasted better than ice cream.

"This is a very good maple thanksgiving,"
she said to Alice.

"Thanks to the maples," said Alice.

"Thanks to the maples," said Mary.